A Little Girl's Guide to
Beauty, Poise and Righteousness

by

Lisa Delmedico Harris

D1512017

HARRISON HOUSE
TULSA, OKLAHOMA

Unless otherwise indicated, all Scripture quotations are taken from The New King James Version. Copyright © 1979, 1980, 1982, Thomas Nelson, Inc.

Scripture quotations marked AMP are taken from The Amplified Bible, New Testament. Copyright © 1958, 1987 by the Lockman Foundation, La Habra, California. Used by permission.

Scripture quotations marked NIV are taken from the Holy Bible, New International Version®. NIV®. Copyright © 1973, 1978, 1984 by International Bible Society. Used by permission of Zondervan Publishing House. All rights reserved.

Scripture quotations marked NLT are taken from the Holy Bible, New Living Translation, copyright © 1996. Used by permission of Tyndale House Publishers, Inc., Wheaton, Illinois 60189. All rights reserved.

13 12 11 10 5 4 3 2 1

The Official Princess Handbook
ISBN: 978-160683-025-3
Copyright 2010 by Lisa Harris
Porum, OK 74445

Published by Harrison House Publishers
P.O. Box 35035
Tulsa, OK 74153
www.harrisonhouse.com

Printed in the United States of America. All rights reserved under International Copyright Law. Contents and/or cover may not be reproduced in whole or in part in any form without the express written consent of the Publisher.

TABLE OF CONTENTS:

CHAPTER ONE

The Princess Ball

Our story starts in a land not too far away, where a little princess was about to awake to a brand new day. Princess Isabella was going to have a very busy day today since all of her princess friends were coming to her castle to attend the Princess Ball. It wasn't everyday that all the other little girls got to visit the castle but this time was different. The king had arranged a ball especially for all the little princesses in the kingdom. Isabella was so excited and could hardly wait to start her day.

Princess Isabella awoke and ran into the kitchen where the chefs were preparing her breakfast. She ate fruit and pancakes with a tall glass of

milk. The castle chef saw that she was almost finished with breakfast and asked her "Did you like your breakfast?" "Yes," she replied with an ill-mannered tone, "but next time I would like whipped cream with my pancakes." The chef wasn't surprised, for Isabella was known in the castle for her unpleasant behavior.

Isabella was known in the castle for her unpleasant behavior.

Isabella's mother walked into the room and overheard the way she had spoken to the chef. "Isabella!" her mother called. "That is not the way to show respect to someone who just cooked you breakfast! Now I want you to apologize and come along with me." Princess Isabella ducked her chin into her chest and said " Sorry, Chef Austyn," and ran out of the room laughing.

Her mother was waiting on her at the foot of the stairs. "Princess Isabella, it is time to start getting ready, you know what today is don't you?"

"Yes, mother," she replied with a long face.

"Aren't you excited that all the other little girls from the kingdom are coming to visit you?"

"I guess" Isabella said. Her mother was confused by the long face and asked Princess Isabella, "If you know what today is then why the long face?"

Isabella burst out with a loud voice, "I don't want all those other girls coming to my castle!"

Her mother wasn't surprised at Princess Isabella's response. "Now Isabella, I want you to go upstairs and start getting ready. It won't be long before we will have company and we have a lot of work to do before the ball."

Princess Isabella did not know what kind of work her mother was talking about but she ran up to her room to get ready for the day. Princess Isabella wanted to get dressed really quickly because she did not want to miss out on greeting her princess friends when

they arrived. So she quickly threw on a dress that had been lying in the floor, slipped on her favorite pair of worn-out shoes and considered herself ready. She didn't even take time to brush her teeth or comb her hair. Princess Isabella looked in the mirror and thought to herself, *No one is as pretty as me,* and ran off downstairs to meet her mother.

When her mother saw her coming down the stairs, she could see that Isabella hadn't taken the time to get ready properly but instead of asking her about her appearance, she simply smiled. She had been trying for weeks to teach Isabella the importance of having good manners and looking her best, but Princess Isabella wouldn't listen. "Come along Isabella," her mother said, "we have a lot of work to do before tonight's ball."

What kind of work is she talking about, Isabella wondered to herself. A princess doesn't have to do work, that's what the maids are for!

As she followed her mother down a long hallway, Isabella began to ask questions, "Where are we going mother? When are the other little girls going to be here? Why do we have to work? I'm tired, can I go play?"

At the end of the hallway Isabella could see someone waiting. As she got closer, she could tell it was Lady Sarah. Isabella was so excited to see Lady Sarah she took off running and jumped into her arms. Lady Sarah was so beautiful and Isabella had always wanted to be just like her one day. "Why Lady Sarah, what are you doing here?" Isabella asked with a loud voice.

"Isabella, stop jumping on Lady Sarah and come over here and stand by me," her mother commanded. But Isabella was so excited she couldn't stop jumping and screaming with excitement. The last time Isabella had seen Lady Sarah was several months ago before she had left to go to a special school.

With embarrassment, Isabella's mother apologized for her daughter's behavior. "This is why I have called for your help," her mother

explained to Lady Sarah.

"Hello, Princess Isabella! It is wonderful to see you too. Have you been a good little princess?" Lady Sarah asked.

Isabella shrugged her shoulders and answered quickly, "Of course, I have. I am always good. Do you like my dress, Lady Sarah?" Isabella asked anticipating a grand reply.

"Well my little princess, it is a little wrinkled and it looks a little dirty."

"Oh well," Isabella announced rolling her eyes, "I was in a hurry to get ready and I didn't have time to pick out a clean one."

"Did you have time to brush your hair this morning?" Lady Sarah asked. "No, I didn't have time and didn't think it was important," Isabella replied. Isabella's mother interrupted and said, "Well, I'm going to leave you two alone so you can get to work. I also have a lot of work to do before this evening's ball," and then she walked away.

CHAPTER TWO

Meet Princess Esther

Lady Sarah wrapped one arm around Isabella and said, "Are you ready to have some fun?"

"Yes, oh yes, yes!" Isabella said jumping up and down again. Lady Sarah took her by the hand and walked to a beautiful couch where they both sat to talk.

"Isabella, your mother has asked me to come and visit you and help you learn some manners."

"Manners! I already have manners. Why do I have to learn more?" Isabella asked.

"You remember when I left last fall for school?" Lady Sarah asked Isabella.

"Yes."

"Well it wasn't just any school I had to go to. It was a very special school called Princess Charm School. My parents sent me there to learn to be a lady."

"But you're already a lady—a beautiful lady! Why would they send you to a school like that?" Isabella asked curiously.

Lady Sarah couldn't help but laugh. "Come closer my little princess and let me tell you a story."

Lady Sarah reached into her bag and pulled out a beautiful book. As she opened it, Isabella asked, "What story? I like stories!"

Lady Sarah began to read…

A long time ago, there was a little princess just like you. Her name was Esther. Esther was a special young lady who lived in the royal

kingdom. She didn't have a mother or father and lived with her cousin Mordecai. Esther was a polite and beautiful young lady and in her heart she had dreams of one day becoming a royal princess. Esther was quiet and polite, well-mannered and very responsible. She made sure she was always well-groomed and looked her best. Esther was a very special young lady who was dear to God's heart—just like you, Isabella!

God showed favor to Esther and her family and He had a wonderful plan for her life. He had destined her to meet the king one day but she didn't know it. It was in her biggest dreams that she only imagined wearing a royal tiara and receiving the king's blessings. In those moments of imagination, she was so excited and hoped that one day her dreams could come true. Little did Esther know that the desires of her heart were about to be granted.

It was a warm spring day and Esther had just gotten out of bed. Her hair still a mess, she made her way to the kitchen for breakfast with her cousin Mordecai. Mordecai loved Esther very much and

had taken her in after her parents were killed in an accident, leaving her an orphan. He raised Esther as his own daughter. "Good morning, my little princess, did you sleep well?" Mordecia asked.

"Yes, thank you," Esther replied.

As Esther made her way closer to her cousin she could see that he was very happy about something. So she asked, "What has caused all your joy this morning? Is there something in your heart to share with me?"

Mordecai sat down beside her and said, "Esther I have known the very desires of your heart for some time and the big dreams you have had of meeting the king and wearing a royal tiara."

"Yes, Cousin but what does that have to do with your joy this morning?" Esther questioned again.

"Mordecai answered, "I awoke to a knock on our door, and as I looked out the window to see who it was, I noticed it was one of the king's men. I thought to myself, *why would one of the king's men be knocking on our door at this time in the morning?* I quickly opened the door to greet him. 'Is this the house of Mordecai, the son of Jair, and the cousin of Esther?' the king's men asked in a loud voice. I replied with the quick answer, 'Yes, sir, it is. I am Mordecai, son of Jair, and cousin of Esther. What can I do for you today?' 'I have been sent by the king to deliver a very special invitation.' He then handed me a rolled up piece of paper. He said 'The king will be sending a royal carriage in the morning,' and turned and walked away before I could thank him."

I stood there looking at the beautifully rolled paper in my hand and stepped back inside then I thought, *why would a royal carriage be arriving in the morning?*

Esther's eyes grew larger with every word and suddenly with a burst of excitement she said, "Oh Cousin, an invitation for me from the king?"

Mordecai smiled and took Esther into his arms and said, "Yes my little princess, just for you." He handed the beautifully rolled paper to Esther. With a gasp of anticipation, she took it from his hand and opened it. She broke the golden seal and carefully unrolled the paper.

Esther rolled up the paper, held it in her hand, and with a solemn look on her face said, "Cousin, I have been chosen by the king to live at the royal palace for the next twelve months. He wishes that I train to wear a royal tiara."

"That is wonderful," Mordecai shouted, "you're going to meet the king! Isn't that what you always wanted?" Mordecia could tell that Esther was not excited about the invitation. "This is a wonderful opportunity and one that you can't pass. God knows the plans He has for you and His plans are to prosper you. He has already prepared a bright future for your life."

To Esther, House of Mordecai

His Majesty requests your presence at the royal palace. You along with other ladies from across the kingdom have been chosen by the King to train for the wearing of the

Royal Tiara

Each lady is required to live in the Royal Palace for twelve months during which she will receive special training.

Your carriage will arrive tomorrow morning at 7 a.m.

Esther replied, "I know, Cousin, I have not forgotten the Holy Word you have taught me but my heart is fearful I might not be all the king desires and I will be gone for twelve months!"

Mordecia took Esther into his arms and told her, "Esther, we must believe you have been called to the royal palace for such a time as this. Don't let the fear in your heart keep you from the wonderful plans God has for you."

Esther was happy and sad. She was happy that her dreams were about to come true but she was also sad that she had to leave the home she had known most of her life. "Cousin Mordecai, you have been good to me. You took me in when I had no place to go, and you have taught me the ways of the God of Abraham, Isaac, and Jacob. For all of these things, I am truly grateful. Twelve months is a long time but I know I must go to the palace."

"Yes, Esther," Mordecai sighed, "it is your time to receive the blessing of the king no matter how long it takes. Don't be afraid my

little princess, it will be ok. We have a lot of work to do before the carriage arrives early in the morning. Let's get started, shall we."

With a smile on her face, Esther answered, "Yes Cousin, I had better get started."

The Official
PRINCESS
Handbook

Chapter Three

Beauty, Poise & Righteousness

Morning light entered her window with the sound of the rooster crowing. Esther knew this was the day and hour she would be leaving home to go to the palace. As she awoke and finally got herself dressed, she went to the kitchen for breakfast and found her cousin waiting on her. He had a gift on the table. "What is it, Cousin?" Esther asked.

"It is a gift for you. Something I have had for a long time but never had the right moment to give it to you." With a smile, Esther reached for the box to open it.

As she pulled away the paper and opened the box, she noticed a beautiful necklace inside. "Oh Cousin, it is beautiful!"

Mordecai was happy that Esther liked the gift. "It was your mother's. Your father gave it to her as a wedding gift a long time ago. I found it in the house after the accident and have kept it ever since."

Esther's eyes' filled up with tears as she pulled the necklace from the box to hold it in her hand. "I will always cherish this moment and this gift. Thank you Cousin Mordecai," she said with a hug.

About that time, a knock on the door broke their embrace. They both knew the knock on the door was soon to follow with a good-bye. It was the king's men announcing the arrival of the royal carriage. "Esther, the time has come for you to go, but this isn't good-bye forever, it is only good-bye for this moment. I will be at the palace gate every day to check on you." Esther's heart was comforted to know her cousin would always be nearby.

Esther picked up her bags to go, hugged her cousin once again and softy said, "Good-bye cousin Mordecai, I will never forget you."

With a feeling of pride in his heart, Mordecai said, "Good-bye my little princess," and kissed Esther on the forehead.

Princess Isabella couldn't believe her ears. She had never heard the story of Esther before and was anxious to hear more. But Lady Sarah shut the book and reached into her bag for another book. "Isabella, do you like the story so far?" she asked.

"Yes but why do we have to stop reading now? I want to know what happens next." Isabella said impatiently. "Would you like to learn what Esther got to learn at the royal palace when she had to stay there for twelve months?"

"OH YES!" Isabella jumped up from the couch and jumped around the room.

Lady Sarah could hardly get her attention. "Princess Isabella, I want you to look at this book with me. It is one of the books I received while I was at Princess Charm School. It is a very special book that I keep with me all the time. It is a guide to help me remember the importance of beauty, poise, and righteousness."

As Lady Sarah opened the book to show Isabella all the pages inside, Isabella asked, "Why does it have so many pages and why is it special to you?"

With a chuckle, Lady Sarah turned and said, "My dear little princess, there is more to being a lady than wearing a pretty dress and having new shoes. This book helps me to remember all the other important things about how to be a lady."

"What important things?" Isabella asked.

"Important things like minding our manners, grooming, and how to take care of ourselves from crown to toe."

Isabella rolled her eyes and said, "Oh no, manners again. I don't understand why I have to learn my manners when I'm already perfect!"

"Perfect? Do you think you're perfect?" Lady Sarah asked.

"Well, maybe not perfect, but I am beautiful."

"Yes, you are. You are special and beautiful. That is why your mother has requested our meeting today. She loves you very much and she knows how the importance of learning to be a lady will help you in the future," Lady Sarah replied.

"I guess I haven't been too nice lately, and I guess learning some new manners won't be so bad. When can we start?" Isabella asked eagerly.

The Official
PRINCESS
Handbook

Princess Manners

Lady Sarah reached into her bag once again and pulled out yet another book. She turned to Princess Isabella and handed it to her.

"Here my princess, I brought you a gift."

Isabella smiled and said, "A gift for me? What is it?"

"It is a book just like mine that helps me to remember the importance of being a lady."

Isabella couldn't believe her eyes. A book just like Lady Sarah's! "Oh, thank you. I love it!"

"I want you to promise me that you will take good care of this book and keep it with you all the time," Lady Sarah explained.

"I will keep it forever and I know right where I will put it." Isabella was so excited and couldn't wait to show her mother. She opened the book to the first page. "Manners Matter," she read aloud. "Lady Sarah, can we look through this book together? Can you teach me what you learned at Princess Charm School? Can you help me learn to be a lady?" Isabella was full of questions.

"Slow down my princess. Yes, to all of your questions but it won't be easy. Are you willing to work hard and practice what you have learned every day?"

"Yes, yes, Lady Sarah. I will, I promise."

"Good then let's get started. The first lesson I want to teach you is how manners matter to a princess."

But as the One Who called you is holy, you yourselves also be holy in all your conduct and manner of living.

1 Peter 1:15

A long time ago in a kingdom similar to this, there was a king who liked to have parties at his palace. He would invite the people of his kingdom to come to the royal palace for a party out in his courtyard.

The gardener worked hard to prepare the courtyard making sure all the flowers and bushes were perfectly manicured. On the day of the party as the guest started to arrive, the gardener noticed how the people were walking on the flowers and destroying the bushes. He became very upset and decided to approach the king with his concerns. The gardener told the king about how rude and disrespectful the guests were and how they had destroyed the courtyard he worked so hard to prepare.

The king was unhappy that the people of his kingdom didn't have manners. So he came up with an idea that he called "etiquette" or little signs that he would use to keep people off the lawn and off the flowers. It was a way to let people know the importance of showing respect to others. The idea was a success. Today, we still use little signs that help us get along with others, like saying "please" or "thank you" or obeying a sign that says "please stay off the grass."

Learning good manners is the first step to becoming a lady. Only you have the power to improve your behavior. If you are unkind and hard to get along with and you are always rude to everyone, people will soon not want to be around you and will consider your behavior ill-mannered. Being ill-mannered is not a label you want to have throughout your life. Being courteous and kind to everyone, including yourself, says a lot about your personality. Your personality also says a lot about who you are. People make character judgments based on the way a person handles herself in social

situations. Always try to be on your best behavior and use good manners at all times.

A person with respect and consideration for others will show and use good manners. Being rude and unkind does not show respect or consideration. God's Word tells us many ways to use good manners. *In First Peter 3:4 NLT it reads, "Clothe yourselves instead with the beauty that comes from within, the unfading beauty of a gentle and quiet spirit which is so precious to God."*

None of us are perfect and we all mess up from time to time, but God doesn't stop loving us because we make mistakes. We should consider our mistakes as lessons learned to help us do better next time. But when we do make a mistake, we should be quick to ask for God's forgiveness.

Love causes you to have good manners. The Bible tells us to love our neighbor as we love ourselves. (Matthew 19:19.) If you have no respect for yourself, you will have no respect for your neighbors. Your neighbors are those people around you including your brothers, sisters, mother, and father. Manners are an expression of love, and love is the greatest expression you can give. Walk in love and practice good manners.

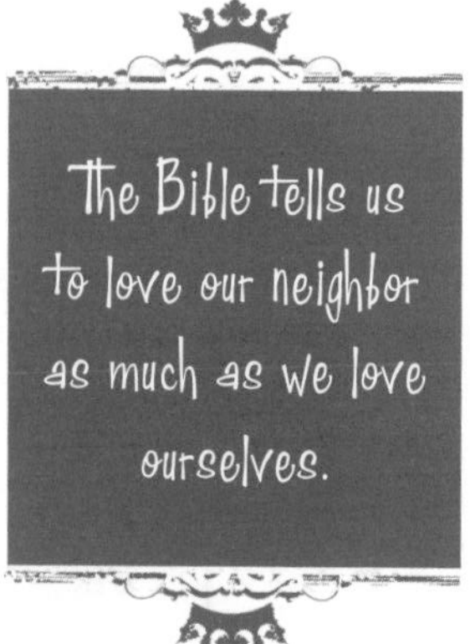

Jesus was always concerned about the well-being of others even in the way He chose to walk among them in perfect behavior. Memorize this scripture and make it your mission to live it: *He who says he abides in Him ought himself also to walk just as He walked. (1 John 2:6.)*

Here are some Princess Crown Thoughts on Manners

Live as children of obedience.
1 Peter 1:14

Let your conversation be gracious and attractive.
Colossians 4:5

Be done with every trace of wickedness.
1 Peter 2:1

Show respect for all people.
1 Peter 2:17

Conduct yourself with honor.
1 Peter 2:12

Keep your mouth from saying evil things.
1 Peter 3:10

Never return evil for evil or insult for insult.
Colossians 4:5

Let your behavior reflect the beauty of your heart.
1 Peter 3:4

Clothe yourself with humility as the dress of a servant.
1 Peter 5:5

Practice hospitality to one another.
1 Peter 4:9

Pursue peace with your fellowman and yourself.
1 Peter 3:11

Love one another for it covers a multitude of sins.
1 Peter 4:8

Everyday Princess Manner Tips

Keep your space clean and neat.

Say "please" and "thank you."

Let others go before you.

Be on time.

Keep your hands clean.

Share.

Knock before entering.

Keep your opinions of others to yourself.

Show respect to your elders by referring to them as ma'am or sir.

Saying, "Excuse me please" is a nice way to say "move."

Push your chair in.

Open it, close it.

Turn it on, turn it off.

Unlock it, lock it back.

If you break it, be quick to admit you were at fault.

Borrow it, return it.

If you value it, take care of it.

Make a mess, clean a mess.

Move it, put it back.

If you don't know how to operate it, ask for help.

If it is not for you to know, then mind your own business.

If asked a question, answer with a kind word and with a soft voice.

If you are yelled at, don't yell back.

Don't repay evil for evil. Instead pray for that person.

CHAPTER FIVE

I Don't Want to Be Rude Anymore!

"Wow!" said Princess Isabella. "I didn't realize there was so much to learn about manners. I thought all you had to do is say 'please' and 'thank you' whenever you wanted to. I had no idea there was so much more."

Lady Sarah chuckled and said to Isabella, "My dear princess, there is a lot to know about manners and how to show kindness to others. My mother and father always taught me to love my neighbor but I didn't really know what they meant until I started watching others. I noticed how rude and unkind people were to one another and I remembered how I didn't like it. I started to look at my behavior

and realized that I was acting just like them—rude and unkind. I didn't like to be told what to do nor did I like to obey my parents, let alone anyone else. I never said 'thank you' or 'please' and I never had time for anyone else. It was all about me. Then I learned that was wrong. I decided I didn't want to be rude any more and that is when I asked my parents to send me to Princess Charm School so I could learn to be a lady of respect and good behavior. You don't have to behave like all the other little girls in your kingdom but you do need to be on your best behavior all the time.

"You see, my dear Isabella, being unkind and ungrateful is not how God has called us to be. It is our responsibility as ladies to display good manners all the time and treat others with the love of Christ. You are not a mistake, but here on this earth for such a time as this, just like Esther. Esther was a polite and kind young lady and because of it, favor was bestowed on her.

"Manners do matter and learning them and doing them are two different things. You can learn proper manners but if you never use

the things you have been taught, then you have not bettered your behavior. God gives us wisdom and teaches us through His Holy Word how we should act and treat others. The Bible is the best etiquette book written.

"Remember, God and people are watching you. Make them proud by the way you choose to behave nicely."

Isabella's face began to turn red with embarrassment as she was reminded of how she behaved this morning at breakfast. "I guess I was rude to the chef this morning when I didn't thank him for my breakfast and then I laughed at him and ran out of the kitchen when my mother made me apologize. I am sorry about the way I behaved."

Lady Sarah was quick to notice Isabella was upset by what she had done. "It's ok, Isabella, we all mess-up sometimes. But the thing to learn from our mistakes is not to make the same mistake twice. In our book, it gives us reminders on how we can be kind and

considerate to others no matter where we are or what we are doing. Let's read them together."

Everyday School Manners

Be on your best behavior even at school. In fact, minding your manners at school is top priority! Follow these simple rules:

- **Respect others—their property, feelings, and authority.**
- **Don't be loud. Use an appropriate tone.**
- **Don't run in the building.**
- **Walk on the right side of the hallway.**
- **Follow school rules without complaining.**
- **Do more than what is expected of you.**
- **Don't interrupt an adult conversation.**
- **Always ask for permission.**
- **Raise your hand and don't blurt out loud.**
- **Show good sportsmanship.**

- Help others when they need help.
- Use time wisely.
- Come to class prepared.
- Be courteous to everyone.
- Don't be a bully and don't be afraid to turn in someone who is.
- Don't be a tattle tail.
- Talk only when you have permission.
- Keep your space neat.
- Keep your chair pushed in.
- Don't stand over someone when they are in conversation with someone else.
- Respect school property.
- Don't slam doors.
- Be nice to everyone, even when they are different than you.

Lunchroom Manners

- Don't cram your mouth full. Chew then swallow.
- Chew your food completely before taking a drink.
- Save talk for after lunch.
- Don't share food or offer it to others.
- Don't comment on other people's meals or their eating style.
- Leave the table clean; pick-up trash even if it isn't yours.
- Stand in line quietly and don't push or shove.
- Report spills or messes to a teacher.
- Use a fork or spoon to eat your food.

School Bus Manners

- Don't scream and yell.
- Stay seated.
- Don't change from seat to seat.

- Don't leave trash on the bus.
- Don't talk to the bus driver when the bus is moving.
- Keep belongings in your seat or next to you.
- Follow the driver's rules.
- Watch for cars when loading and unloading.
- Keep your feet out of the seat and center aisle.
- Help watch out for others.

Princess Phone and E-Etiquette Manners

- Consider your tone and the loudness of your voice when talking.
- Be respectful in public places like meeting halls, school, church, restaurants, movie theaters, or in a store.
- Turn phone on silent or off when in a quiet place.
- Don't text when you are walking in a public place.
- Keep your eyes on where you are going.
- Don't make prank calls.
- Take a break from the computer and phone.

- **Don't let electronic devices control you.**

- **Say hello and identify yourself to a caller.**

- **Don't hang up on someone.**

- **Only call 911 in an emergency.**

- **If you send emails, make sure they are short and to the point and use the subject line for details.**

- **If someone emails you remember to reply to them promptly.**

Showing Special Kindness

Thank You Notes

A thank you note is a great way to show appreciation. When sending a thank you note, make it personal by using your own handwriting. A thank you note should be sent within a week's time. Don't wait a month to send it.

There are many reasons to send a thank you note. Send a thank you note when someone gives you a gift, does something nice for you, helps you complete a task or job, takes time out of their

schedule to help you, when you are invited to a party, or when you stay at a person's home for more than two days.

There are many ways you can show appreciation and say thank you. It says a lot about a person's character when they take the time to say thank you.

How to Be Thoughtful to Others

Everyone is worthy of a nice gesture. Learn to go out of your way to be kind to others. A card, phone call, or a simple hello is a great way to help brighten someone's day.

Think of others and treat them as you would like to be treated. It is nice to keep a list of your friends' and family's birthdays, anniversaries, and special occasions handy. Prepare ahead of time cards or letters to send. Keep special occasion cards on hand like thinking of you, you're the greatest, thank you, you're special, and holiday cards. Christianity is about loving one another and giving to others.

Eating Like a Princess

"The next few tips are about table manners," Lady Sarah explained. "I have an idea! How about we learn table manners over lunch?"

Isabella loved that idea, for she hadn't eaten since breakfast and happily replied, "Yes, I'm starving!"

"Good, then it's settled. Let's have lunch." The castle chef had already prepared a special lunch for Isabella and Lady Sarah—spaghetti and meatballs, salad, and garlic bread. Soon lunch was served in the parlor where they had been all morning.

“Before we begin our meal, I want to teach you about all the dishes on the table and what to do with the napkin and all the silverware. Once you are seated, take the napkin and lay it across your lap. Don’t tuck it into your shirt like a bib or leave it lying on the table.

“In front of you, you will find a large dinner plate. On the right-hand side of the plate, you will see a knife and a spoon. The knife is to be used to cut your dinner meat or even your lettuce. The spoon is used for your soup, or in this case, to help twirl your spaghetti onto your fork. Your water glass and dinner beverage will always be on the right side. On the left side of your dinner plate, you will find two forks, one smaller than the other. The smaller one is to be used for your salad and the larger one is to be used for your dinner meal.”

“Do I use the larger fork first and what about the two smaller plates to my left, what are they for?” Isabella asked.

"The smaller plate without the knife is your salad plate and the one with the knife is your bread plate. You also have a spoon directly above your dinner plate. This is your dessert spoon." Lady Sarah continued to explain, "Learning table settings can be overwhelming at first but when you understand it from the beginning it isn't so hard. Remember these simple dining do's and don'ts."

The Do's and Don'ts of Table Manners

- **Don't lick your fingers.**
- **Don't burp aloud.**
- **Don't remove food from your teeth with your fingers.**
- **Don't talk with your mouth full.**
- **Don't make a scene when you see something in your food that shouldn't be there—remove it quietly and without comment.**
- **You may ask the waiter for another serving.**
- **Don't squeeze a lemon wedge without first shielding it with your hand.**

- Don’t wrap your napkin around your neck.
- Don’t make a big mess.
- Don‘t forget to push your chair in.
- Don’t hug your plate.
- Don’t put your elbows on the table.
- Don’t double dip.
- Do place your napkin in your lap.
- Do leave the lemon wedge in your glass.
- Do leave your napkin in your chair if you plan on returning to your meal.
- Do ask to be excused from the table.
- Do use your silverware for non-finger foods.
- Do sit up straight in you chair.
- Do taste foods before adding extra seasoning.
- Do thank the cook, waiter, or host.
- Do eat over your plate.
- Do start using your silverware from the outside and work your way in.

Formal Place Setting

1. Napkin
2. Water Glass
3. Tea Glass
4. Bread Plate
5. Bread Knife
6. Soup Bowl
7. Soup Spoon
8. Dinner Plate
9. Salad Plate
10. Salad Fork
11. Dinner Fork
12. Dinner Knife
13. Dessert Spoon
14. Coffee Cup
15. Saucer

Isabella was so excited to learn more about manners and Lady Sarah was such a good teacher. But she couldn't help but wonder about the story of Esther, so she asked, "Lady Sarah, can we

read more about Esther when we are through with our meal? I think I need a break from all this manner stuff."

With a laugh, Lady Sarah replied, "Of course, we can!"

They both finished their spaghetti and garlic bread and couldn't wait to try the raspberry cheesecake for dessert. "Chef Austyn has done a wonderful job preparing our lunch today, don't you think Isabella?" Lady Sarah asked. "I think we need to do something special for him."

Isabella 's eye's widened, she had an idea. "Can I make him a thank you card, Lady Sarah, and will you help me?"

"I think that is a wonderful idea Isabella. Giving a thank you card is a way to show you are thankful. It also is a great way to show kindness and good manners."

As they made their way back to the couch, Lady Sarah reopened the book of Esther and continued to read.

Don't Be Afraid!

As the carriage disappeared over the hillside, Esther clutched the necklace around her neck thinking about all the things that had happened in her life. She was grateful for her cousin Mordecai and for the many blessings in her life. She also thought about how she had never been away from home and how she had never seen the royal palace. *I bet it is a beautiful place,* she thought to herself.

She could see the castles' rooftops growing nearer and nearer. She thought to herself, *I hope the king likes me and I find favor with him.* In next to no time, the carriage had arrived at the

castle's gate. The king's men opened the gate and trotted the horses up to the door. "My lady, we have arrived. No need to worry about your bags, they will be waiting for you in your room.

"Thank you." Esther replied with a soft voice.

Esther was amazed at the beauty of the palace. It was just as she had imagined. Soon she was greeted by a lady dressed in a servant's attire. "You must be Esther, niece of Mordecai. I have been expecting you. Please follow me as I show you to your quarters." Esther walked after her, still in amazement of the beauty that surrounded her. "My name is Elisabeth and I have been assigned to you as your personal servant for the next twelve months.

Twelve months, Esther thought again to herself. It seemed like eternity. "What a pleasure it is to meet you, Elisabeth."

"Let's get you to your quarters so you can get unpacked and rested before lunch," Elisabeth said with urgency in her voice.

“Consider it an honor to be chosen by the king. Not every young lady is given the opportunity to live and learn at the palace.”

“I am very grateful for this time,” Esther replied.

Elisabeth took Esther down a long hallway in the castle and showed her where she would be staying. “This is one of the best rooms in the palace. The king had it prepared especially for you, Esther.” The splendor of the room captivated Esther’s imagination and took her back to those times she had dreamed of living in a royal palace. “Lunch will be served at 11A.M. I will come for you when it is time. Get some rest and make yourself at home,” Elisabeth commanded. But Esther was too excited to rest or even think about unpacking. She could only imagine what would happen next.

Within what seemed like a very short time, Elisabeth was back to take Esther to lunch. “The king’s eunuch is waiting in the

ballroom. He will explain the king's invitation and what will be required for the next twelve months before the crowning ball."

Esther followed along quietly as she listened to every word. *Don't be afraid my little princess,* she was reminded in her thoughts as she entered the ballroom. Seated around a beautiful long table were other young ladies just like her.

As Esther found her seat, a tall, handsome man entered the room. "Hello ladies, my name is Hegai. I am the king's eunuch and in charge of the ladies quarters. You have been invited here by the king and chosen from many in the kingdom. For the next twelve months, each of you will be given beauty preparations and classes on how to be a royal princess. After twelve months of preparations, each of you will meet the king. If the king finds favor with you, you will receive his blessings along with the royal crown." Esther was amazed and could hardly believe she was having lunch at the royal palace.

Princess Isabella was eager to hear more but Lady Sarah had once again stopped reading. “ Isabella, do you think Esther went to the royal palace in a wrinkled dress with her hair un-combed?”

Isabella looked down at her dress and replied, “No. I guess I need to pay more attention to my clothes and how I take care of myself.”

“The next lesson Esther would have learned during her twelve months at the castle was how to take care of herself from crown to toe. Let’s open our book to the next lesson on Princess Grooming,” said Lady Sara.

Princess Grooming

I will praise You, for I am fearfully and wonderfully made; Marvelous are Your works, and that my soul knows very well.

Psalm 139:14

You are fearfully and wonderfully made. God has taken the time to create everything about you—from the sound of your voice, to your unique smile and laugh and even to your unique one-of-a-kind fingerprint! That is amazing but what did you expect—God Himself is amazing. If God has taken the time to create you, don't you think it should be important to take care of His creation?

Grooming, like manners, involves a lot of hard work and attention. You have to pay attention to your body. Washing and combing your hair is one way to take care of your body. But there are many things to know about grooming. In the Bible, our body is referred to as a holy temple; the very place where the Holy Spirit dwells. First Corinthians 6:19-20 NIV tells us, *Do you not know that your body is a temple of the Holy Spirit, who is in you, whom you have received from God? You are not your own; you were bought at a price. Therefore honor God with your body.*

God Himself uses our body as a dwelling place for His Spirit, making our body sacred, holy ground. If our body is a temple for the Lord to dwell, we should be proud of it and keep it clean, well-groomed, and in good shape. Our temple, or body, should be cleaned and maintained daily, inside and out.

As a princess, your body is important to God. Without your body, how would He accomplish His purpose and see His glory

in the earth? God needs your hands, your feet, and every part of you in order to help carry out His perfect plan. How would you feel if you walked into your church building and noticed the wallpaper coming down, light bulbs burned out, the floor dirty, and everything dusty? You would think the person in charge did not care much about the building and taking good care of it. That is how it is with your body. When others see you, what do they see? Do they see someone who is well-groomed?

God invested time, love, and creativity into creating you and it is your responsibility to invest time in taking care of His creation. You are important! You have the fingerprints of Christ all over you. Do not abuse your temple. Love you and your body. When taking good care of yourself consider your entire body inside and out—what you eat and drink and how much exercise you get everyday, and even how many times you take a bath. God made you body, soul, and spirit, and all these parts are important.

Now let's talk about how to take care of your body from crown to toe. Beauty is more than bathing, grooming your hair, and putting on beautiful clothes. Beauty comes from the inside, and taking care of you means you work on not only how you look but also how you feel.

Your body won't shape-up by itself nor will it stay clean all the time, you will have to take care of it. It will never be perfect, no matter how hard you try to make it perfect. Jesus is the only perfect creation. But you have to take care of your body before it will take care of you. Do not forget you have been created wonderfully and fearfully in the image of God. Take care of what God has skillfully and uniquely created.

How to Take Care of a Princess

A princess should bathe at least once a day to keep her body looking beautiful, clean, and smelling fresh. Proper cleansing is the most important thing you can do for yourself. A clean,

fresh smelling body is more appealing than a quart of the most expensive perfume.

Bathing is simply a combination of water, soap, and a little bit of scrubbing to remove the dirt, oil, and perspiration from your body. Washing your body with water and soap is a great way to stay clean and smelling fresh. Either a shower or bath will do, but no matter which you prefer, don't forget to use the soap! Use it to work up a good rich lather on a sponge or washcloth--any soap is better than none. Lather yourself well all over. Use a long handled brush for those hard to reach places. Don't be afraid to scrub. Brisk scrubbing is good for your skin as it loosens oil and dirt. Don't forget to scrub your fingernails, elbows, toes, heels, the soles of your feet, and behind your ears!

Now that you have properly cleansed your body, rinse well with warm water. Dry yourself with a clean towel and don't forget to clean-up your mess and put dirty clothes in the hamper. This is a way to show respect and use good manners as well.

There are many products that can help you keep smelling and feeling fresh all day, products like lotions, perfumes, and deodorants (if you are old enough). If you like to wear perfumes, remember a little bit goes a long way.

Exercise

Watching the foods you eat and exercising will help you stay healthy and feeling great. A little exercise every day, no matter what kind, is always good for your body. Sitting in front of the television or lying around listening to the radio, will not benefit you. God made your body to be on the move. Think about it; everything on the inside and on the outside of you is constantly moving. So use your body the way God intended it to be used. Shake off that laziness, pull yourself up off that couch and away from the TV, throw out the junk food, and get to moving. Make a difference for your body's sake.

Proverbs 19:15 reads, *Laziness casts one into a deep sleep, and an idle person will suffer hunger.* The best way to stay in shape is to

get moving and to eat healthy food. Be happy with who God has made you to be and take care of His creation.

Skin

Skin comes in many colors. In the beginning, when God created man and woman, we are not told what color of skin they had, and it really doesn't matter. They were made in the image of God, and God's skin color is beautiful. No matter if you were born black, white, red, or yellow, it is all beautiful in God's eyes. However, like your personality, your skin is your own. You have the power to determine the appearance and beauty of your skin by the way you choose to care for it. Take care of your skin and protect it. It is never too late to start a daily facial routine.

Wash your face, morning and night, with a bar of soap. Make sure to choose a gentle soap for this task.

Washing your face and body with a simple washcloth is a great way to exfoliate and remove deep down dirt and grime.

After washing your skin and patting it dry with a clean towel, use a mild liquid astringent to remove dirt build-up. Apply with a clean cotton ball and rub gently.

Lotion is a great way to protect your skin and add moisture where needed.

Do's and Don'ts of Skincare

• Do keep your hands off your face as much as possible. Your hands house oils and bacteria and oil and bacteria, cause problems for your skin. Make it a habit to wash your hands regularly.

• Do wash your face twice a day, morning and night. Stay on schedule with your facial cleansing routine. Your skin collects grit and grime throughout the day and it settles into your pores. Even though you may not see dirt, there is hidden dirt that needs to be removed.

• Be very careful when out in the sun. The sun dries out your skin. Wear protective covering and lotions when you have to be in the direct sunlight. Protect your skin as much as possible.

• Do keep lip balm on your lips to keep them moist and beautiful.

• Do drink plenty of water to cleanse your skin to keep it glowing.

• Don't pull or tug on your skin. Instead, use a gentle touch.

• Don't take your skin for granted. It won't take care of itself.

Hair

God loves you so much that He has taken the time to decide the color of your hair, the color of your eyes, how your smile should look, the uniqueness of your voice and laugh, and even

the placement of dimples on your cheeks. He has skillfully designed your every feature. Think about this, God loves you so much that He even has the very hairs on your head numbered! Yes, your hairs are numbered! Can you believe it? That is amazing! Use these simple rules when caring for your hair.

It is important to wash your hair at least every other day with clean water and shampoo. Put a small amount of shampoo in your hand and rub your hands together to create a lather. Then use your fingertips to lather up your hair. Rinse with clean water.

When combing, avoid tugging on your hair when it is wet or dry. Use a wide toothed comb or pick to comb when it is wet.

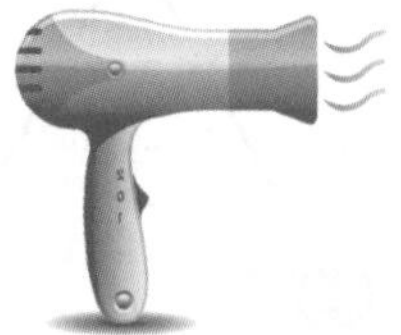

The key to great hair is taking care of it. Heat can damage your hair so it is best to avoid pointing the dryer directly on your hair.

Teeth

Do you brush your teeth every day, morning and night? If you do not, then you should. A princess would never leave home without brushing her teeth. Your smile is one of a kind and you only get one set of teeth in your lifetime. Take care of them.

Hands

Do you ever get tired of hearing your mother say, "Don't forget to wash your hands!" Well, she is right. Listen to your mother or whoever is telling you to wash your hands. Your hands touch many things throughout the day and on those things are germs! In order to remove those germs, you must wash them off. Using hand sanitizer is ok when there is no soap and water available, but soap and water is always better. Keep your hands and your nails clean. A princess always takes good care of her hands and her nails.

Do's and Don'ts of Nail Care

• Do keep the dirt clean from under your nails.

• Do keep lotion on your hands and feet to keep them moist.

• Do ask for help trimming your nails until you learn to do it yourself.

• Do use a small, stiff brush to scrub your nails.

• Do keep your nails neatly shaped.

• Don't forget your toenails.

• Don't use your nails as tools.

• Don't bite or pull loose nails .

• If your mom or older sister helps you to paint your nails, be sure to keep the polish nice and neat. If the polish is chipped, ask them to help you repair it.

• Don't bite your nails--toenails or fingernails.

Princess Posture

Princess Isabella was listening to every word. "Lady Sarah, I never knew that learning my manners could be so much fun. There is a lot to learn, isn't there?" Isabella asked.

"Yes, my little princess, there is. I never knew there was so much to learn about manners either. I am glad you think learning your manners is fun and I am glad to be your teacher," Lady Sarah replied softly, "and we still have more to learn. Are you ready to continue?"

Princess Isabella leaped off the couch and said, "Yes!"

Lady Sarah began, "Not only did Esther learn about manners and grooming, she also learned about posture."

"What is posture?" Isabella asked curiously.

"Let's read our lesson on Princess Posture and find out, shall we?" Lady Sarah began to read.

Princess Posture

> *He who says he abides in him ought himself also to walk just as he walked.*
>
> *1 John 2:6*

Good posture can show self-confidence and can speak a lot about how you feel about yourself to others.

The Bible is full of many scriptures that teach us the proper way to walk, talk, sit, dress, behave, and live. For example, Romans 13:13 tells us to walk properly, and not in lewdness, lust, strife or envy. God expects you to walk with confidence, in righteousness, in peace, and in His commandments and

ordinances. If you walk in God's ways it will help keep you from slouching.

Loving yourself is the key factor in having great posture. When you feel great about yourself and your confidence is on the high, you cannot help but stand upright. It is that Princess Power, the power of the love of Jesus in your life, helping you love yourself and others around you. Without it, you cannot have great posture. Without love, nothing works. Love yourself, value yourself, and respect yourself. Give yourself a hug and say aloud in front of a mirror, "I am good! I can stand up and stand tall in Christ Jesus!"

Your posture is not only important in the way you sit, stand, and walk naturally, but it is also important to know how to sit, stand, and walk spiritually. Correct posture in Christ means that we understand the power that we have in Him. God has given us everything that pertains to life and godliness. (1 Peter 2:3.) We have been given authority over the powers of darkness and all that it brings. (Luke 10:19.) We have been given power through the blood of Jesus, through the Word of God, and by His powerful name. Sickness is under our feet. Everything bad that is found in Deuteronomy 28 is under our feet. We have been redeemed from the all of the bad stuff. (Galatians 3:13.)

You have been given all that Christ has been given. You are Christ on this earth. Hold your shoulders back and your head high and walk with the confidence of knowing the power of Christ Jesus in you. Stand tall and strong, daughter of the King!

Here are some Princess Crown Thoughts on Posture

Always stand up straight and tall and avoid slouching your shoulders.

Your body language says a lot about who you are.

Good posture takes practice.

There is always someone watching you. Set a good example for others to follow.

Practice good posture no matter where you are.

When walking, keep your chin up and your eyes focused on where you are going.

Sit up straight and tall in your chair with your hands pleasantly placed in your lap.

When getting in and out of a car, sitting or standing remember to keep your ankles and knees close together.

When stooping to the floor, always bend at your knees and keep your back straight.

When carrying heavy books or bags remember to switch arms to lighten the weight.

A princess always takes notice of how she enters and exits a room.

A princess doesn't compromises her position in Christ.

The Official
PRINCESS
Handbook

How to Look Like a Princess

"Look at me, Lady Sarah!" Isabella had jumped up from the couch and was prancing around the room. "Is this the way you walk gracefully?" Isabella asked, waiting for Lady Sarah's reply.

"Well look at you! You've been listening haven't you? I'm so proud of you. YES! You are walking with poise and grace. What will your mother say when she sees what you have learned?"

"She will say, 'Princess Isabella, you are magnificent!'

Lady Sarah couldn't help but laugh. Soon they were both prancing around the room laughing. Isabella bumped into Lady Sarah and gave her a big hug. "Lady Sarah, thank you for teaching me my manners. This has been a grand day."

"My little princess, the day has just begun." Lady Sarah hugged Isabella and they both sat down on the couch. "You have learned a lot, Princess Isabella, and I am proud of you. But we must complete one more lesson before you can say you have officially completed Princess Charm School. And don't forget the story of Esther. We have to find out what happens at the end."

"I think Esther was beautiful, just like you, Lady Sarah." Isabella said with a smile.

As Lady Sarah opened the handbook to the next lesson, Isabella asked, "What are we going to learn about now, Lady Sarah?"

"I'm going to teach you how to dress like a princess," Lady Sarah explained.

"Dress like a princess?" Isabella looked at her dress and said, "I already know how to dress like a princess."

Lady Sarah couldn't help but giggle. " Isabella, I want you to look at your dress and tell me if you think Esther would have wanted to wear it to lunch at the royal palace?"

Isabella looked down at her dress again and replied, "I guess she wouldn't like the wrinkles or the stains. I was in a hurry this morning when mother asked me to get dressed. I didn't have time to find a clean dress."

Lady Sarah began to explain the importance of dressing like a princess to Isabella. "Princess Isabella, I want you to pay close attention to this lesson."

How to Dress Like a Princess

Charm is deceitful and beauty is passing, But a women who fears the Lord, she shall be praised.

Proverbs 31:30

In the world today, there are many fashion designers and beautiful clothes to wear but who are you letting determine your style and the clothes you wear?

If you know anything about clothes then you should know that they have been created to cover the body. In our society, it seems that idea has changed. Don't be fooled by the idea that it is ok to show your skin in public. It isn't ok.

God does care about how you dress. You are a representation of His son Jesus Christ. Therefore, what you wear should reflect what is inside.

There are many ways you can dress both stylish and modestly. Dressing to expose yourself is not attractive. There are areas

of your body that are meant to be covered. Don't pattern your fashion style after the pop star on the cover of a magazine. Be yourself by creating your own style.

Wearing clothes is a way to express who you are. You may be a jean and t-shirt kind of girl or you may be someone who likes to dress up. No matter what your style, make sure it is created with the ideas of God in mind. You should dress appropriately for God, not as a requirement, but out of respect for Him and others. You can cause others to stumble by the way you choose to act, speak, or the way you dress.

You should stand out in a crowd, not blend in. The Bible tells us, *I beseech you therefore, brethren, by the mercies of God, that you present your bodies a living sacrifice, holy, acceptable to God, which is your reasonable service. And do not be conformed to this world, but be transformed by the renewing of your mind, that you may prove what is that good and acceptable and perfect will of God.* (Romans 12:1-2.) You have been called to stand out and make

your own fashion statement. Jesus is the only fashion designer who can help you develop a style that is right for you. Don't let the world influence the way you dress or even your friends. When it takes two shirts to cover your top, then wear them. Don't bare it all for the sake of style. In fact, showing skin isn't fashionable at all. The way you dress speaks a lot about what you think of yourself. If you care about who you are and what you look like, then you will take the time to dress with respect and modesty.

People look at your outward appearance and judge you based upon what they see, but God looks at your heart and sees someone made beautiful through the works of Jesus. (1 Samuel 16:7.) Don't place your value on the clothes you wear. You can wear all the name brand fashions and expensive shoes to match, but clothes won't get you anywhere. Especially if they are dirty.

Dressing like a princess involves knowing how to care for your clothes. A princess never leaves home without looking her

best. She makes sure her clothes are clean and free from stains, pressed and presentable. Here are some tips to help you keep your wardrobe looking its best.

Dressing Like a Princess

• Keep your clothes neat and clean.

• Keep your shoes polished and clean by washing them often.

• Ask your mom to have a Mr. Clean erase pad on hand for stubborn stains.

• If a garment needs to be mended— ask your mom to mend before wearing it.

• Keep your delicate stockings in a zip lock bag.

• Keep your accessories clean, including your handbags and hair bows.

• Ask your mom to wash out stains as soon as they happen.

• Express yourself in a modest and attractive way.

• Find a style that reflects your lifestyle.

• Don't wear something that would cause someone to stumble.

• God looks at the appearance of your heart. How is it dressed?

Looking Like a Princess

• Smile.

• Look friends and adults in the eye.

• Stand-up straight.

• Hold your chin up and your shoulders back.

• Walk with confidence.

• Don't hide behind your hair Always dress the part.

• Keep your nervous habits to yourself (fidgeting, biting nails,

playing with your hair, swinging your foot, etc.).

• Be grateful for any compliments you may receive.

• Let Jesus shine through you.

• Walk in love.

• Have respect for the feelings of others.

• Speak to everyone.

• Call people by their name.

• Be friendly and helpful.

• Be generous with your praise and be cautious with your criticism.

• Avoid hurtful words.

• Be interested in the lives of others.

• Be ready to help without being asked.

- Always have a kind word to say.
- Keep your opinions and attitudes to yourself.
- Practice good manners.
- Walk in the fruit of the Spirit.
- Do what you say you will do.
- Never speak out of turn.
- Always be ready to share the good news of Jesus!

Beauty is in the Total Package

Beauty is found in the total package, from crown to toe, and from heart to soul. True beauty comes from the attitude of the heart. Here are some things the Bible tells us not to wear:

> A negative attitude, envy, anger, grumpiness, bitterness, a lying tongue, ungratefulness, sadness, a frown, unkindness, disrespect, gossip, selfishness, rudeness, fear, jealousy, a filthy mouth, pride.

Lady Sarah closed the handbook and held it close to her chest.

"Lady Sarah, is there something wrong?" asked Isabella.

“Not at all my little princess, my heart is full of gratefulness from what I have learned at Princess Charm School. I am honored that I can share what I have learned with you today. There are people who love you very much and they care about the way you should behave. It isn’t ok to be rude and unkind to others or even disobey your parents. I used to be unkind, rude, and didn’t even care if I brushed my hair or teeth, but now I understand the importance of being a lady and how it can help me live a better life. Esther had to stay at the royal palace for twelve months in order to learn the ways of the king. I had to stay away at school for twelve months to learn to be a lady. That is why the story of Esther is so dear to me and I have chosen to share it with you. Would you like to find out what happens to Esther?” Lady Sarah asked Isabella.

“Yes! Isabella shouted with excitement.

Esther spent the next twelve months preparing to meet the king. All the other young ladies in the palace also trained

beside her, but Esther was different. She grew in beauty, poise and grace and found favor with all who saw her. Esther had not forgotten all the things her cousin Mordecai taught her. Her faith in God kept her strong and full of confidence and she knew it was because of her faithfulness that the favor of God was upon her. Mordecai checked on her every day at the palace gate as he had promised.

Each young lady chosen from the kingdom had their chance to meet the king. Finally the day had come and it was Esther's turn. This was the moment she had been waiting for. All the dreams she once had when she was a little girl were about to come true. She couldn't believe she was about to stand before the king.

Esther was taken to the king's palace where the king was waiting on her. The king saw Esther and loved her more than all the other young girls and she obtained grace and favor in his sight. So he set the royal crown upon her head and made her queen of the kingdom.

The king made a great feast, and called it the Feast of Esther. Esther did wonderful things for her kingdom and her people and there was no doubt that she had been put in the place of royalty for this certain time.

CHAPTER TWELVE

The Feast of Isabella

"So you see my little princess Isabella, wonderful things are waiting in your future. God has a special plan for your life just as he had a plan for Esther's,' Lady Sarah explained.

Interrupted by a knock on the door, Isabella could hear her mother's voice call, "Isabella, it's time to get dressed for the ball, your guests will be arriving soon." Isabella jumped off the couch with a leap and ran to the door. She embraced her mother with the biggest hug she had ever given. "Did you have a good time with Lady Sarah today, Isabella?" her mother asked hugging her back.

"Yes Mother, oh yes, thank you! I am so glad you invited her here today. Lady Sarah taught me how to be a lady and how important it is to mind my manners. I have learned so much and Lady Sarah is a wonderful teacher!"

Her mother was amazed at Isabella's response. She had only hoped that Lady Sarah could help Isabella with her manners. She never dreamed Isabella would be this excited. "Thank you Lady Sarah," Isabella's mother said with a smile.

"It's time to get ready for the ball, my little princess. The guests will be arriving soon and we want to greet them at the door," Isabella's mother explained.

"I know just what to do!" shouted Isabella. She ran upstairs in a hurry, jumped in the shower, brushed her teeth and fixed her hair. She even put on a clean dress! "No more dirty dresses for me," she said to herself, "and I'll never forget to brush my hair again, I'm a princess!"

It was time for the guests to arrive and Isabella walked gracefully downstairs to meet her mother. "You look beautiful, Isabella! I'm so proud of you," said Mother.

As the guests entered the door, Isabella greeted them with kind words, "How do you do? How are you? It is a pleasure to meet you. Thank you for coming." Her mother couldn't believe how the afternoon with Lady Sarah had changed Isabella's behavior.

The guests had arrived and everyone gathered in the royal ballroom. The palace chefs served dinner and Isabella was excited to use the table manners that she had learned from Lady Sarah. *The small fork is for salad, the large fork is for dinner,* she thought to herself.

The king would be arriving soon and all the little princesses of the kingdom were excited. It would be their first time to meet the king. As the meal was being served, a loud trumpet sounded announced the king's entry into the ballroom. Everyone stood to their feet and praised his glorious beauty.

As the king made his way to the table, he stopped to make an announcement, and silence fell on the room. “Tonight is a special night, it is a princess ball. For each of you are special in the kingdom and all of you have found favor and grace in my sight, but tonight I would like to honor a special princess,” he said with authority and power. Everyone looked around the room wondering who he was talking about. “It is someone with whom I am well pleased.” He paused for a moment and announced, “Little princesses of the kingdom, welcome to the Feast of Isabella.”

Isabella had no idea her father had planned a special ball just for her. She stood to her feet and bowed in thankfulness and then walked over to her father’s side. He placed a beautiful crown on her head and kissed her on the forehead. “You have come to a position of royalty for such a time as this,” her father said with a prideful heart. The room quickly filled with clapping and cheering. It was a grand night at the ball.

Pancakes with Whipped Cream

The next morning Isabella awoke to the sun shining in her window. She couldn't wait to run downstairs for breakfast. She brushed her teeth and fixed her hair, chose a clean dress from her closet, and slipped on her favorite slippers. She also grabbed a pink piece of paper from her dresser and hurried downstairs to the kitchen. The castle chef had prepared her favorite breakfast—fruit and pancakes with a tall glass of milk and this time the pancakes had whipped cream!

Chef Austyn saw that Isabella was almost finished with breakfast and asked her, "Did you like your breakfast this morning?"

“Yes,” Isabella replied with a smile.

Chef Austyn was surprised at Isabella’s kind words. Isabella finished her breakfast, cleaned up her mess, wiped her mouth with her napkin, pushed her chair in and started to leave the room when Chef Austyn noticed she had left something on the table.

Isabella you left your pink paper on the table,” he said. Isabella turned around, smiled, and said, “I know,” and walked up stairs to her room.

Chef Austyn was puzzled by Isabella’s behavior and picked up the paper to see what it was.

> To: Chef Austyn, you’re the bestest chef in the whole wide kingdom, thank you for pancakes with and without the whipped cream.
>
> Love, Isabella.

Declaration of a Royal Princess

I declare on this the (date)__________day of (month)______________ in the year of our Lord Jesus (year)__________, I (name)______________________________ accept who I am and who God has made me to be. I vow to learn to love myself the way God has made me. I will behave like a royal princess no matter where I am or what I am doing. I will take this Royal Princess training and apply it to my life. I will be a doer of the Word of God and will believe all of it. I will make Jesus my vital necessity and serve Him with all my heart all the days of my life.

I declare I am a divine design and I am full of great potential. God has a plan and purpose for my life and He has given me everything good. God loves me. I have been created in the image of God—a King's Daughter entitled to the blessing and benefits of salvation through Christ Jesus.

I am a Royal Princess!

Date:____

Princess:______________________________________

Princess Charm School Insructor:____________________

About Princess Charm School

If you are interested in learning more about Princess Charm School, please visit our official website at www.princesscharmschool.com or write to us by email at lisa@princesscharmschool.com.

Prayer of Salvation

Father, I believe that Jesus died on the cross for my sins. I believe that He rose from the dead so I can live with Him forever. I ask You to forgive me of my sins. I ask You to come into my heart and be the Lord of my life. I confess with my mouth that I am born again. Thank You for saving me. Amen.

About the Author

Lisa Delmedico Harris is the founder of Princess Charm School and has been involved in the fashion, modeling, and pageantry industries since her pre-teen years. A wife and mother of three, Lisa has a heart desire to teach others about the true meaning of beauty.

The Harrison House Vision

Proclaiming the truth and the power

of the Gospel of Jesus Christ

with excellence:

Challenging Christians to

Live victoriously,

Grow spiritually,

Know God intimately.

Other Books by

Lisa Delmedico Harris

Princess Charm School:

A Godly Approach to Beauty, Poise, and Righteousness

By Lisa Delmedico Harris

Paperback: 6x9 • 288 Pages
$21.99
ISBN #: 978-1-60696-624-2

Product Catagory: JUVENILE NONFICTION Girls & Women RELIGION Christian Life Women's Issues

True beauty is having Jesus on the inside, so his qualities show on the outside.

Society has set in motion a false idea of beauty that focuses only on outward appearance and completely overlooks the heart and soul of a person. Princess Charm School: A Godly Approach to Beauty, Poise, and Righteousness will guid readers through the pressures of our modern world while offering sound advice about beauty, etiquette, posture, and other tips, combined with relevant wisdom from God's word.

Teens and preteens will love Lisa Harris's Princess Charm School, which proves to them that only from God's wisdom can they start to grow and mature into a beautiful woman of God. Our natural beauty will fade like the flowers and grass, but it is the quality of a gentle, beautiful spirit that will live and last forever.

www.princesscharmschool.com